Henrietta Hexagon & the TRIANGLES

A note from the Author:

"First of all, I would like to thank God for giving me the gift of being able to write and illustrate for children. I want to thank my daughter Blayke for helping me decide how to draw Henrietta and giving me great ideas to use throughout the story. I want to thank my 3 kids and nephews for donating their artwork to use on Henrietta's walls. I also want to thank Brandi, Apryll and Michele for taking time to look over my book before sending it to print. Last but not least, I'd like to thank my family for being so supportive of everything I do."

Check out other books by this author as well:

Henrietta Hexagon was a happy little shape with SIX beautiful sides.

As an infant, she was left in a shape sorter with no one to care for her.

Luckily, she was found by the nicest parents ever, Ma and Pa Triangle.

They took her home to their little square cottage on Groveland Circle. She was adopted and became part of the triangle family along with three brothers and a sister named Tate, Tanya, Tanner and Tyler.

Groveland Circle

Henrietta loved her family more than anything but she always felt like she never quite fit in.

One warm spring morning, Henrietta woke and quietly crept into the den careful not to wake the others. She was happy to find Ma Triangle sitting on the couch knitting a rectangle scarf.

Henrietta plopped down beside her and said, "Ma, can I ask you something?" "Sure honey," Ma replied. "What seems to be the problem?" "Why am I so different? There are circles, triangles, rectangles, ovals, and squares everywhere you look but there are never any hexagons."

"Oh, sweetie," said Ma. "It's ok to be a little different, that's what makes you special. There are hexagons everywhere too. You may just have to look a bit harder to find them." Henrietta wasn't quite convinced that she was special but she hugged her Ma. "Thanks Ma, I love you," she said and hurried off in search of hexagons.

First, she had to gather some supplies to help her with her search. She ransacked her toy box and found a net, binoculars, and a magnifying glass.

Unfortunately, nothing she found was in the shape of a hexagon. The toy box was a rectangle, the binoculars and magnifying glass were made with circles, and the net was made up of little diamonds.

Not ready to give up yet, Henrietta threw the net over her shoulder and hurried outside. Surely she would have better luck out there, right?

In the meantime, Ma had come up with a plan to show Henrietta how special she really was. As soon as Henrietta left the cottage, Ma jumped off the couch and darted upstairs to wake Pa and the kids to tell them about her plan.

Back outside, Henrietta wasn't having much luck. She managed to find one hexagon but it had gotten her into quite the mess.

She stumbled upon
a nest of bees and was surprised to find that
their home was made up of tiny little
hexagons. She was only trying to get a closer
look when a bee flew out and stung her right
on the nose!

Trying to escape, Henrietta spun around
too quickly and slipped in the honey that
had dripped on the ground.

17

She managed to pull herself up and
made it safely to the nearest pond.
She dove in just in time without
getting stung again, but she had lost
all of her supplies.

Wet and sticky with her hair all a mess, she decided to call it a day and head home. When she reached the front door, all the lights were out. "Well, at least everyone is still asleep and won't see what a mess I've made of myself," she muttered under her breath.

She opened the door and turned on the light. "Surprise," yelled her family. Henrietta rubbed her eyes and gave herself a quick pinch to make sure she wasn't dreaming.

Her entire family of six triangles had all come together and were in the shape of a hexagon! "See Henrietta," Ma said, "you do fit in."

"You are so special that it takes six of us to make just one of you," Pa added. Tate, Tyler, Tanner and Tanya all said together, "We love you sis!"

From that point on, Henrietta knew she was the perfect fit. She was the happiest shape alive!

2477012R00013

Made in the USA
San Bernardino, CA
26 April 2013